# Benjamin Franklin

Published in the United States of America by Cherry Lake Publishing
Ann Arbor, Michigan
www.cherrylakepublishing.com

Content Adviser: Ryan Emery Hughes, Doctoral Student, School of Education, University of Michigan
Reading Adviser: Marla Conn MS, Ed., Literacy specialist, Read-Ability, Inc.
Book Design: Jennifer Wahi
Illustrator: Jeff Bane

Photo Credits: © Internet Book Archive Images/Flickr, 5, 7; © Everett Historial/Shutterstock, 9, 21; © One for All: A Pennsylvania Number Book, Sleeping Bear Press, 11; © Sarony & Major/Library of Congress, 13; © USCapitol/Flickr, 15; © C. Brothers, N.Y., 1882/Library of Congress, 17; © Dan Thornberg/Shutterstock, 19; Cover, 8, 14, 18, Jeff Bane; Various frames throughout, Shutterstock Images

Library of Congress Cataloging-in-Publication Data

Names: Haldy, Emma E. | Bane, Jeff, 1957- illustrator.
Title: Benjamin Franklin / by Emma E. Haldy ; illustrated by Jeff Bane.
Description: Ann Arbor : Cherry Lake Publishing, 2016. | Series: My itty-bitty bio | Includes bibliographical references and index.
Identifiers: LCCN 2015026236| ISBN 9781634704786 (hardcover) | ISBN 9781634705387 (pdf) | ISBN 9781634705981 (pbk.) | ISBN 9781634706582 (ebook)
Subjects: LCSH: Franklin, Benjamin, 1706-1790--Juvenile literature. | Statesmen--United States--Biography--Juvenile literature. | Scientists--United States--Biography--Juvenile literature. | Inventors--United States--Biography--Juvenile literature. | Printers--United States--Biography--Juvenile literature.
Classification: LCC E302.6.F8 H314 2016 | DDC 973.3092 [B] --dc23
LC record available at https://lccn.loc.gov/2015026236

Printed in the United States of America
Corporate Graphics

**About the author:** Emma E. Haldy is a former librarian and a proud Michigander. She lives with her husband, Joe, and an ever-growing collection of books.

**About the illustrator:** Jeff Bane and his two business partners own a studio along the American River in Folsom, California, home of the 1849 Gold Rush. When Jeff's not sketching or illustrating for clients, he's either swimming or kayaking in the river to relax.

I was born in 1706.

My father made soap and candles.

I had sixteen brothers and sisters.

I was good at reading. I liked to write.

What do you like to study?

I trained to be a printer. I made books. I made newspapers.

I also liked to invent things. I studied **electricity**.

I wanted to make my town better.
I helped set up a fire department
and a library.

I became postmaster general.
I made sure everyone got
their mail.

Do you like visiting the library?
Why or why not?

I lived in America. We were ruled by the king of England.

We were not happy about how the king treated us. We wanted to be free from him.

I joined other leaders to declare America's **independence**.

We went to war for freedom.

We needed money and help.

I went to France. I got support for our war.

We won the war.

I helped set up our new country.
I helped write the **Constitution**.

I lived a long and full life. I died of old age.

I was an extraordinary man. I was smart and curious. I helped found America.

What would you like to ask me?

1746

1700

Born
1706

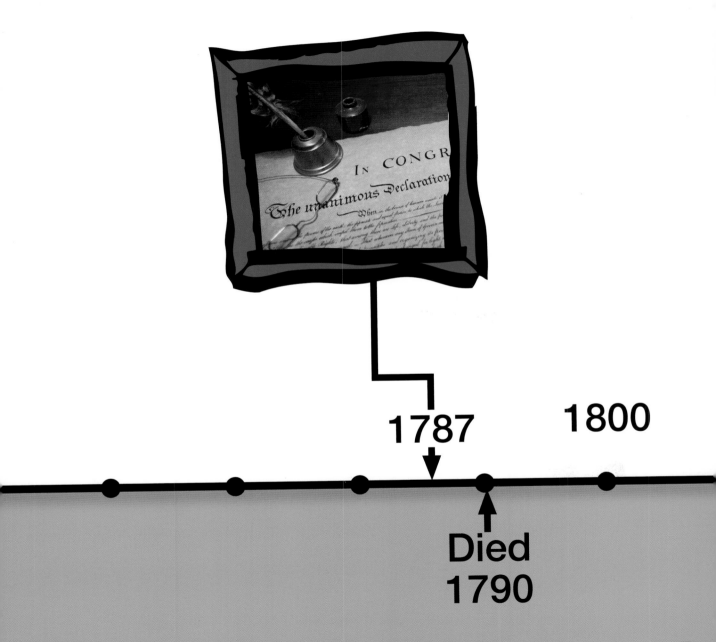

1787

1800

Died
1790

## glossary

**the Constitution** (THUH kahn-sti-TOO-shuhn) the document that explains the laws and organization of the U.S. government

**electricity** (i-lek-TRIS-i-tee) energy that powers lightbulbs and other things

**independence** (in-di-PEN-duhns) freedom

## index